100-YEAR-OLD TORTOISES!

By Leonard Atlantic

Gareth Stevens
PUBLISHING

Please visit our website, www.garethstevens.com. For a free color catalog of all our high-quality books, call toll free 1-800-542-2595 or fax 1-877-542-2596.

Cataloging-in-Publication Data

Names: Atlantic, Leonard.
Title: 100-year-old tortoises / Leonard Atlantic.
Description: New York : Gareth Stevens Publishing, 2017. | Series: World's longest-living animals | Includes index.
Identifiers: ISBN 9781482456202 (pbk.) | ISBN 9781482456226 (library bound) | ISBN 9781482456219 (6 pack)
Subjects: LCSH: Testudinidae–Juvenile literature.
Classification: LCC QL666.C584 A43 2017 | DDC 597.92'4–dc23

Published in 2017 by
Gareth Stevens Publishing
111 East 14th Street, Suite 349
New York, NY 10003

Designer: Andrea Davison-Bartolotta and Bethany Perl
Editor: Ryan Nagelhout

Photo credits: Cover, p. 1 USO/iStock/Thinkstock.com; pp. 2–24 (background) Dmitrieva Olga/Shutterstock.com; p. 5 Lauren Pretorius/Shutterstock.com; p. 7 Nneirda/Shutterstock.com; pp. 9, 11 Aekkaphum Warawiang/Shutterstock.com; p. 13 Ricard MC/Shutterstock.com; p. 15 Nick Dale/Shutterstock.com; p. 17 Darrin Henry/Shutterstock.com; p. 19 Fotos593/Shutterstock.com; p. 21 Jess Kraft/Shutterstock.com.

Printed in the United States of America

CPSIA compliance information: Batch #CW17GS: For further information contact Gareth Stevens, New York, New York at 1-800-542-2595.

CONTENTS

Boldface words appear in the glossary.

Slow and Steady

Tortoises are slow-moving animals. They walk slowly, they eat slowly, and they sleep many hours of the day. But they're some of the longest-living animals on Earth. These **reptiles** can live more than 100 years. Some live much longer!

5

Tortoises are much like turtles and **terrapins**, which are also reptiles. The main difference is that tortoises spend all their time on land. And unlike turtles, tortoises can't swim, and most only eat plants.

On the Shell

Tortoises have a hard, rounded shell called a carapace (KEHR-uh-pays). It's made of bony plates. The carapace helps keep the tortoise safe from predators. The hard scales on a carapace are called scutes (SKYOOTS). They help make the shell stronger.

SCUTES

Rings?

Many people think you can count the rings on a tortoise's shell to find out its age. But most tortoises' rings go away when they become an adult. The only way to know a tortoise's age is to know when it was born!

11

Tortoises on the Island

The Galápagos Islands in the Pacific Ocean are home to tortoises that can live over 100 years. The oldest known Galápagos tortoise lived to be 152 years old! They're the largest tortoises on Earth. They can be 5 feet (1.5 m) long and weigh 550 pounds (250 kg)!

Galápagos tortoises eat flowers, grass, leaves, and cactus. They like to lie in the sun and can sleep over 15 hours a day! Their body can store water and food so they can go up to a year without eating or drinking.

CACTUS

Jonathan

Jonathan is a giant tortoise said to be 184 years old. Jonathan is 2 feet (0.6 m) tall and 3.75 feet (1.1 m) long. He was a gift to the governor of Saint Helena, an island in the South Atlantic Ocean. Jonathan arrived in the late 1800s!

Lonesome George

In 2012, a Galápagos tortoise named Lonesome George died. He was thought to be over 100 years old! George was the last Pinta Island tortoise, a special kind of Galápagos tortoise. People tried unsuccessfully for over 30 years to find George a **mate** so Pinta Island tortoises wouldn't go **extinct**.

19

Endangered Tortoises

Some of the longest-living tortoises, such as Galápagos tortoises, are **endangered**. Many people once ate these tortoises because they were easy to catch. Today, they need our help to stay safe! People need to be careful to protect tortoise eggs and not harm their **habitats**.

GLOSSARY

endangered: in danger of dying out

extinct: no longer existing

habitat: the natural place where an animal or plant lives

mate: one of two animals that come together to produce babies

reptile: an animal covered with scales or plates that breathes air, has a backbone, and lays eggs

terrapin: an animal with a hard shell that lives in both freshwater and salt water

FOR MORE INFORMATION

BOOKS

Black, Vanessa. *Tortoises*. Minneapolis, MN: Bullfrog Books, 2017.

Hirsch, Rebecca E. *Galápagos Tortoises: Long-Lived Giant Reptiles*. Minneapolis, MN: Lerner Publications, 2016.

Riggs, Kate. *Tortoises*. Mankato, MN: Creative Education, 2016.

WEBSITES

Galápagos Tortoise
animals.nationalgeographic.com/animals/reptiles/galapagos-tortoise/
Learn more about tortoises here.

Giant Tortoise
worldwildlife.org/species/giant-tortoise
Find out more about giant tortoises on this World Wildlife Fund site.

INDEX